FADING ADS OF
LONDON

FADING ADS OF
LONDON
HELEN COX

First published 2014

The History Press
The Mill, Brimscombe Port
Stroud, Gloucestershire, GL5 2QG
www.thehistorypress.co.uk

British Library Cataloguing in Publication Data.
A catalogue record for this book is available from the British Library.

ISBN 978 0 7524 9762 4

Typesetting and origination by The History Press
Printed in India

CONTENTS

ACKNOWLEDGEMENTS

Special thanks to Sam Roberts of ghostsigns.co.uk, John Rymer of Ghost Signs UK and @Dakota_Boo on Twitter. Between them they have provided valuable information on the location and history of adverts across the city. They have also provided a great deal of support and encouragement while I have been completing this volume.

Many thanks to my publisher, The History Press, for commissioning a book on this rather obscure strand of social history.

Most of all, thanks to my fiancé, Jo Pugh, who has reignited my love for history and encouraged my writing. He has also endured an incalculable number of hours of standing about in all weathers while I photographed and catalogued fading adverts across the country – for this he deserves much credit.

ABOUT THE AUTHOR

Helen Cox was raised in Thirsk, North Yorkshire. After completing her Master of Arts in Literature and Creative Writing, she moved to London to pursue a career in writing. She has since written about a range of cultural topics for publications such as the *Guardian*, *The Spectator* and Film4.com. She is currently editing *New Empress Film Magazine* whilst finishing her first novel. For more information on the author visit helenography.net.

INTRODUCTION

At its core, London is a city in constant structural flux; an ever-evolving mass of glass and steel that shifts with the demands of contemporary design. Beyond the blaze of neon lights and the banshee shrieks of braking red double-deckers, however, an older city survives. Its rugged, brick visage, weathered with character and history, is yet to be given a smooth, concrete facelift. It is in these forgotten nooks that faded adverts of old slowly, silently decay. These adverts, sometimes called ghost signs or brick adverts, come and go with the churn of commerce and often all that is left is some carefully painted, spectral lettering. This book is a catalogue, of sorts, of the adverts currently visible in London. By the time you finish reading, some of the lettering you have read about may have been lost forever and new examples are likely to have been unearthed.

Faded signs are a living history of Britain's businesses, marketing and media. Although some people consider marketing a relatively recent societal development, entrepreneurs and brands have been paving the way for the new media generation for hundreds of years. Just as Adidas or Go Compare might spend money on a prominent billboard placement today, brands such as Bovril and Criterion Matches would, in the early 1900s, commission hand-painted adverts in noticeable positions across the capital. Although there are many exceptions to this rule, prime locations for spotting examples of faded adverts are next to railway stations and on high streets; main thoroughfares that see a lot of footfall. Such spaces granted companies the maximum amount of exposure for their investment and are still used by brands today – it is not uncommon to see faded adverts and billboards next to each other, or to see billboards covering old brick adverts. While some of the faded ads in London can be found on the sides of buildings where those same businesses once operated, it is more frequently the case that advertisers went for prominence over proximity to their premises.

Faded brick signage survives most flagrantly in areas that have had little post-war development. Photographs from the 1920s suggest that ghost signs were once commonplace all over the city. The area around Blackfriars Bridge, for example, was once awash with signs for newspapers and journals due to its proximity to Fleet Street. Some of the adverts on Fleet Street itself still survive, but the area by the river has seen so much demolition, redesign and repainting that the hand-painted signage once found on every available flat surface no longer exists in this area.

Many of the advertisements featured in this book are hand painted. Such adverts are not exclusive to London, or even Britain. This is partly because signage too has its own wider history; separate, though connected to that of branding, and hand-painted brick signs are just one small segment of the signage story. The first known photographs of hand-painted brick adverts appear in William Fox Talbot's Parisian street scenes of the 1840s. Wall-chalking (drawing adverts in chalk on walls) had by this time become popular after the banning of hanging signs in 1762 due to injuries and deaths caused by poorly secured signs falling on pedestrians. Painting onto brick, rather than chalking, was a natural progression and in America a rise in commercialism before the Great Depression made such signs very popular. The sheer number of these faded adverts still in existence, both in London and further afield, suggests that hand-painted promotions were popular for a significant length of time; these signs were, after all, created by individual artists working from paint tins, and such craftsmanship is time-consuming.

Understanding the nuances and deeper significance of faded adverts is not purely a matter of being able to identify old brands that have long since vanished from the shelves of shops and household cupboards – although admittedly that does help. It also requires some degree of decipherment, which may mean revisiting the same image again and again until some sense can be made of it. Those interested in faded adverts become keen interpreters of lettering that is so faint that it is almost impossible to read. They also become experts at picking out words from multiple layers of adverts: there were only so many prominent places to situate adverts across the city and consequently the same spots would be reused. As the signs have faded, their under layers have been revealed and this effect is commonly referred to as palimpsest by faded signs enthusiasts. The term palimpsest originally referred to old scrolls or books that were scraped clean for reuse and the word has since been adopted by the architectural community to reference layers of design. Distinguishing a particular design based on one or two letters is no easy job, but this is often the key to uncovering the background to a company that everybody else has long since forgotten, which in turn offers insight into trends and historical consumer behaviour.

Helen Cox, 2014

I

PROMINENT
BRANDS

440–442
Romford Road, E7

In 1843, Francis May and William Bryant formed a Provisions Merchants partnership called Bryant & May Ltd on Tooley Street in London. In 1850 they struck upon the idea of importing Swedish matches from Carl and Johan Lundström, two important figures in the commercialising of safety matches, and within three years were selling over 8 million boxes of Brymay matches annually.

269 Lillie Road, SW6

It is unsurprising that so many Bryant & May adverts survive, as they were most forward-thinking when it came to their promotional strategy; in 1899 they backed what is now considered to be the first animated commercial. Created by British filmmaker Arthur Melbourne-Cooper, 'Matches: An Appeal' featured stop-motion matchstick men, made of actual matchsticks, writing messages on a chalkboard. These messages encouraged the audience to donate one guinea, a sum which would enable Bryant & May to send a free box of matches to every British soldier fighting in the Boer War.

9 Kings Parade, W12

Bryant & May were not so revolutionary in terms of their policies on employee rights. An article entitled 'White Slavery in London', by women's rights activist Annie Besant, fanned the flames for one of the most notorious strikes in London history. The article brought to light the health hazards of working with white phosphorus, the exhausting fourteen-hour shifts and the unjust fines on wages. Ultimately, this exposé sparked the London matchgirls' strike of 1888.

Bow Quarter, Arlington Building, E3

The former Bryant & May factory in Bow still stands today. It was built in 1911, closed down in 1979 and has, like most empty premises in the capital, since been converted into flats. This was the site of the matchgirls' strike and, before Bryant & May used it for the production of matches, the grounds were previously used to manufacture candles, crinoline and rope.

232 Kilburn High Road, NW6

This sign is an example of a palimpsest (multiple visible layers of lettering). The type for Gillette razor blades reads: 'Buy Gillette Safety Razor. British Made.' Type is also visible for Soviet-manufactured Criterion safety matches. It reads: 'Criterion Matches. Great Gift Scheme. Save the Packet Labels.' Criterion customers could collect matchbox

labels and exchange them for gifts: 100 labels could be exchanged for 7lb of fruit bonbons, while 1,500 labels would buy either a guitar or 1lb of Russian caviar.

113 Stoke Newington Church Street, N16

With this similar example of a palimpsest it is possible to see lettering for the *Westminster Gazette* as well as the Gillette and Criterion matches. The *Westminster Gazette* was founded in 1893 and merged with the *Daily News* in 1928. This dates all of the adverts for this publication somewhere within that thirty-five-year bracket.

41–43 Willesden High Road, NW10

In 1901 King C. Gillette invented the first safety razor. It was granted a patent on 15 November 1904. He employed a range of advertising techniques during these early years, including print adverts and editorial promotion, and went from selling 51 razors and 168 blades in 1903 to 90,000 razors and 12 million blades in 1904.

Bayswater Underground Station, 89 Queensway, W2

Some of the remaining Gillette signs use imagery to sell safety razors. This example of a father and daughter is reminiscent of images one might expect from twenty-first century television adverts for shaving.

43 Stamford Hill, N16

In this palimpsest, lettering is visible for both the *Westminster Gazette* and Army Club cigarettes. The *Westminster Gazette* was a leading liberal evening newspaper that published the early works of Rupert Brooke, D.H. Lawrence and Raymond Chandler. Army Club cigarettes were produced by Cavanders (acquired by Godfrey Philips Ltd in 1961) and, alongside Carreras' Black Cat cigarettes, were a niche tobacco brand in the early twentieth century.

56 Holloway Road, N7

This building dates back to 1900 when it was used by bootmaker Warrell Joseph. By 1906, however, Mark Wallis hairdressing took over and locks have been chopped at this address for over a hundred years since. Army Club may have chosen this spot for advertising due to the number of men visiting the barbers; when Percy William set up a tobacconist at No. 60, also in 1906, purchasing cigarettes after a cut would have been quick and convenient.

126–138 The Broadway, Muswell Hill, N10

Although this sign is mostly obscured by a billboard, the khaki background colouring of the advert is very much in keeping with the colouring of other advertising for the Army Club brand. Promotional materials for Army Club play, as the name suggests, on imagery relating to army propaganda and masculinity.

104 New Cross Road, SE14

This sign boasts traces of lettering for Criterion matches, Redfern's rubber mats and Nestlé milk. The Nestlé slogan reads: 'Richest in Cream'. This was one of their most popular advertising slogans and was used on a range of printed, painted and enamel adverts.

515 Wandsworth Road, SW8

Behind the billboard, this sign encourages mothers to use Nestlé's milk if they can't feed their babies themselves. Such infant formula products have a surprisingly chequered history: Nestlé products were boycotted in the 1970s and '80s when people felt that the firm's 'aggressive marketing' in the third world was leading to the product being mixed with contaminated water. Food giant Danone were also attacked in June 2013 over their marketing campaign in Turkey, which suggested that mothers weren't providing enough milk for their children and should use their supplement.

761 Wandsworth Road, SW4

Redfern's Rubber Works was in business for over a hundred years. Originally founded in 1900 by Wilfred E. Redfern, the company began by producing rubber heels for boots and shoes in their factories at Hyde, Cheshire.

Redfern's were understandably keen to make themselves a household names and consequently embarked on their first major advertising campain in 1910. Their adverts were printed in both newspapers and magazines and, to demonstrate that the company was on its way up, Mr Arnold H. Redfern was sent to London a year later.

Redfern's played a part in both the First and Second World Wars. Between 1914 and 1918 they manufactured the mouthpieces for army-standard gas masks, and during the Second World War they produced rubber components for the fighter planes. In the late 1960s the company merged with H.G. Miles to form Miles Redfern Ltd, which eventually closed in 2006.

13 Bonnington Square, SW8

In the 1880s, speciality breads appeared on the consumer market and, by 1912, a range of bread brands had been established. Judging by the adverts that they left behind, two of the most competitive brands were Daren and Hovis. Both of these brands advertised on the walls of bakers such as this one. Bay's Bakers was listed at this address between 1937 and 1953.

173 Queen's Road, SE15

Daren was originally registered as Keyes Daren Mills Ltd on 30 December 1908. They lasted a considerable length of time – almost seventy years – before going into voluntary liquidation in August 1972. After this they became part of what is now Rank Hovis McDougall.

60–62 Stoke Newington Church Street, N16

Daren used a mixture of wheat, rye meal and wheatgerm in their product and were keen to promote the health benefits of their bread. This is a line taken by many brands at the time as there was no advertising legislation to deter them from making false promises to their customers. Bakers that have traded at this address include William Kennedy in 1906 and Dick Thomas Kennedy (probably his son) who took over in 1926.

26 Palace Gates Road, N22

Hovis used several strategies to promote their product. Firstly, they made it known that their flour formula was patented and therefore exclusive. They then further emphasised in their adverts that they were the bread of choice for the Royal Family – it was well known that Queen Victoria herself was a fan. Just like Daren, Hovis were also keen to note the health benefits of their product.

26 Knight's Hill, SE27

The faded text on this sign reads: 'Hovis Bread: the World's Best, the Hygienic Bakery Famous for pure Devonshire Bread. Catering and Contracting in all its Branches.' Like many other bakeries at the time, the word 'hygienic' was used in the advert, perhaps reflecting a general fear of disease.

94 Northcote Road, SW11

Dunn Bakers are listed at this address between 1934 and 1948, meaning that the sign is a lot newer than some might think; a lot of literature about faded advertisements place them in the late nineteenth and very early twentieth centuries – not so with this sign and, thus, possibly others. Both Daren and Hovis were absorbed by Rank, a business that originated with Joseph Rank's flour milling enterprise. The company is now owned by the conglomerate Premier Foods.

Effra Road, SW2

Bovril was invented by Scotsman John Lawson Johnston. He famously won a contract to supply 1 million tins of beef to the French army in the 1870s but was unable to meet demand. Consequently, Johnston's Fluid Beef was born – later renamed Bovril. Somebody who is likely to have sold Bovril on this patch is Mrs Caroline Medwi, who was a grocer here in 1926.

679B Romford Road, E12

Though this sign and the advert on Effra Road were clearly commissioned solely for brand awareness purposes, Bovril bigwigs were quite edgy in the early years. They caused uproar in the 1890s by releasing an advert featuring Pope Leo XIII holding a mug of Bovril. The slogan simply read: 'Two infallible powers: The Pope and Bovril.'

185 Fleet Street, EC4A

This sign features a place rather than a brand. Dundee is famously known for its 'jute, jams and journalism'. The Dundee *Evening Telegraph* was founded in 1887 and is the sister paper to the *Courier*, which was first printed in 1801 as the *Dundee Courier & Argus*. Both titles are still in print.

66 Notting Hill Gate, W11

This is a sign for Dundee jams, or marmalade to be more specific. It is often alleged that Janet Keiller of Dundee invented marmalade in 1797. Though much older recipes are on record, Keiller's marmalade – inextricably associated with Dundee – became famous, and can still be found today. Sadly there are currently no faded adverts in London for Dundee jute, but new signs are uncovered every day.

123A
Blackstock Road, N4

William Hesketh Lever and James Lever launched Sunlight Soap in 1885. It was produced in Port Sunlight, their factory across the river from Liverpool. The Victorian era was a good time to be setting up business in the hygiene trade, as people were plagued by germs and ill health. The soap was designed to be accessible and affordable, even for the working class.

122 Villiers Road, NW2

Port Sunlight became a model village that accommodated the workers of the Lever Bros firm. It still stands today on the Wirral peninsula and is home to 900 Grade II listed buildings. The Lever Bros, seeking to expand and develop their business, merged with other companies and became Unilever. Some Sunlight cleaning products can still be found around the world today.

77 Mitcham Road, SW17

This sign is for Player's Navy Cut cigarettes. John Player, born in Essex in 1839, came to Nottingham in 1862 and set up shop on Beastmarket Hill. There he sold manures, seeds and pre-wrapped tobacco. The tobacco was so popular it became his main source of income and consequently, in 1877, he bought William Wright's tobacco factory in the Broad Marsh area and opened two more shops.

31 Kenworthy Street, E9

This advert sports the famous 'Player's Please' slogan. By the time John Player died in 1884 he owned a further three factories, all of which produced tobacco. The business was tended by close friends until his two sons, John and William, were old enough to take over in 1893. The business became a private limited company in 1895 with a share capital of £200,000.

97 Uxbridge Road, W12

This advert for the Player's Navy Cut brand is very faded but it is still possible to decipher the price of the cigarettes on the top left and lower right corners respectively: ten for 6*d* and twenty for 11*d*.

A closer look reveals some of the lettering, which is still visible alongside the outline of the sailor who had the names of various ships emblazoned across his cap, including the HMS *Invincible*. The Player's factories were demolished in the late 1980s and the brand now belongs to the Imperial Tobacco Company.

2

CENTRAL LONDON

Tisbury Court, WID

There are several stunning elements to the design of this advert for the tailor, at No. 2 Little Crown Court. The company's specialist area appears to be providing workwear for waiters, as the faded lettering reads 'The noted house for waiters, cafe jackets, dress coats, trousers, vests and all articles & wear for hotel employees.'

A closer look reveals that the advert is also translated into French. Due to the fading it is quite difficult to make out but 'De tous genres pour garçons de café et tous les articles pour employes d'hotel' clearly has a very similar meaning.

The black and white nature of the illustration, with just dashes of flesh colour for the waiter's hands and face, would have helped to keep the cost of the sign painting down. London saw an increase in the number of French residents in the aftermath of the Franco-Prussian War and the Paris Commune at the start of the 1870s.

42 Amwell Street, EC1R

Although the signage at No. 42 reads Lloyd & Son, their dairy was originally listed at No. 54 from 1916 onwards. The building's business listings show that there was a gap in 1941, and by 1942, Lloyd's bakery were listed at No. 42.

The reason for the move from No. 54 to No. 42 is likely to be due to bomb damage from the Second World War. This area was heavily bombed during 1940 and 1941. When the Lloyds – the family who ran the dairy – moved to this address, they no doubt invested in new frontage, so this signage is likely to date from the early '40s.

Look down at the step leading into the building and you will also see this surviving mosaic. The nearby avenue, named Lloyd Baker Street, is not connected with this business, but instead references the Lloyd Baker family who owned the land in the 1700s.

319 Gray's Inn Road, WC1X

George Herbert bought a scale-making business owned by George Birch at this address in 1857. He was the son of Thomas Herbert, who founded Herbert & Sons. They are listed at this address as late as the 1940s. In 1948, however, the business here was deemed unprofitable and, although the Herbert family stayed in the scale business, somebody else took over scales sales at this address.

Austin Friars Passage, EC2

Pater & Co. are listed at No. 53 New Broad Street in the 1930s. As their sign states, they were stock and share brokers. A small manicule (pointing hand) shows potential customers the way to their door.

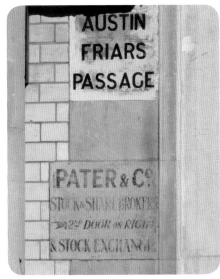

231–232 Strand, WC2R

The Aerated Bread Co. Ltd are listed in business directories from the 1930s. Their head office was at No. 17 Camden Road, while their maintenance department was located at No. 100A Theobald's road.

They were a substantial business and had bakeries, stores, warehouses and depots listed at Fleet Street, Kentish Town, Holborn Viaduct and Fenchurch Street amongst many others.

55 Sidmouth Street, WCI

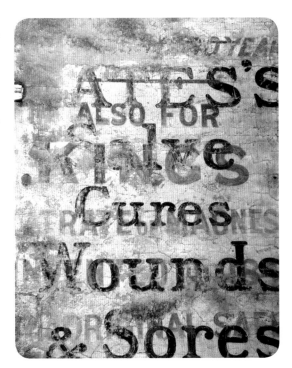

Bates & Co. were listed at this address in the 1930s and early 1940s. They were manufacturers of Citrate of Magnesia, which was believed to have health benefits. By the end of the Second World War, however, they were no longer in the area.

A closer look at the lettering in this advert gives clues to some of the supposed healing qualities of Citrate of Magnesia: 'Cures Wounds & Sores.'

148 Curtain Road, EC2A

C. & M. Davis Ltd are listed at 145–150 Curtain Road in 1921. They worked in the wholesale upholstery industry.

NCP Car Park Great Eastern Street, EC2A

Mr David Meyer founded the Meyers Bros Parking System Inc. in the early 1920s. By the 1960s the company provided parking for over 25 million cars in America and the firm clearly had some success over here too. In 1964 the company was sold to The Hertz Corporation.

88 Old Street, EC1V

It is fitting that the most famous faded sign for the Salvation Army sits east of Central London, as this Christian denomination and charity was originally founded in Whitechapel in 1865. By 1910 the organisation had over thirty premises listed around London, including a shelter for women on the nearby Hanbury Street. The building on Old Street continues to be used for charitable purposes, as it is now used by the homeless charity Shelter.

22 Dingley Road, EC1V

Walk round to the rear of this building and you will see a faded advert for Black Cat cigarettes. This particular brand of cigarettes was produced by Carreras Tobacco Company. Their biggest competitors were Imperial Tobacco and British American Tobacco.

180 Euston Road, NW1

The factory in which Black Cat cigarettes were produced (now called Greater London House) still stands. Although the Carreras tobacco business began in the eighteenth century, the Black Cat cigarette was not introduced until 1904 and their art deco building on Euston Road was not completed until 1928. It is considered an exemplar of early twentieth-century design and, with its two black cats guarding the doorway, it is difficult to miss.

198–208 Old Street, EC1V 9BP

This advert not only remembers a lost business but a lost borough of London. The parishes of Clerkenwell and St Luke's formed the borough of Finsbury in 1900, which existed until 1965, when it became part of the borough of Islington. Finsbury Van & Wheelworks existed to the rear of where No. 196 Old Street now stands.

67 Monmouth Street, WC2H

This sign has been restored, which is why the lettering is so easy to read. It betrays Monmouth Street's rather mixed reputation during the Victorian era. It may have catered to those from the upper classes with shops such as this one, but it is also the site of several unsolved murders, as the police allegedly didn't deem the victims of enough importance to investigate.

3
NORTH
LONDON

79 Shepperton Road, NI

Warings was a company listed in the 1920s on London Wall. They manufactured women's underclothes in Wilton Factories.

107 Essex Road, NI

Broad Yard underwent a name change in 1938, becoming Essex Road. Hatters and hosiers were commonplace around London at this time, as the wealthy bought their clothing from specialist retailers.

22 Cloudesley Road, N1

The red lettering in this advert is difficult to read, but on closer examination it says 'Wooton's Cash Chemist'. The advert seems to be in two parts which could suggest that one was added at a later date. This pharmacy was owned by Joseph W. Hearle who also owned two other pharmacies in Islington.

27 High Street Islington, N1

This building was once Lockharts Ltd cocoa rooms from the late 1800s until 1912, when the business changed its name to Lockharts Ltd refreshment rooms. By 1925, however, it had been converted into a hatters. Though this sign is faded, it is possible to just decipher the name. The business belonged to G.A. Dunn.

69 Graham Street, N1

In 1926 the sole proprietors of Diespeker & Co. Ltd are listed as R.O. Bryen and Charles Dodd. Their address is listed as No. 60 Holborn Viaduct, where a towering glass structure built by KPF architects now stands. Diespeker was a mosaic and tile manufacturer. They also supplied fireproof flooring and partitions and had a base at Dowgate Wharf on Upper Thames Street. There is little history left in this area due to the Blitz and the post-war redevelopment; it is likely that the company moved to Graham Street to continue business after the war.

214 Camden High Street, NW1

By 1912 Boots were already claiming to be 'the largest, best, cheapest retail chemists in the world' in the trade directories. By the 1930s they boasted over 200 branches in London and the suburbs. The chemist still thrives on the British high street today.

Greenland Place, NW1

Miller Beale & Hider were listed at No. 162 High Street, Camden Town in the 1930s. As the advert is so well preserved, it is likely that the company touched it up regularly or used a lead-based paint, which is much more durable.

From a distance it is also possible to appreciate the fact that their signage spanned the top of their building. This may suggest that the surrounding buildings were either lower at the time of painting or weren't even built. An advert at that height would be plainly visible to passengers on local double-decker buses and trams.

258 Pentonville Road, N1

This building has a rather odd and convoluted history. In the late 1800s it was used by Alfred Pilgrim, who was a sausage maker. By 1926 Mrs Fanny Pilgrim was running the business – possibly Alfred's widow. In 1933 the premises was converted into a restaurant owned by A. Smith & Son, and in 1936 it was used for hairdressing. Now, as this picture illustrates, it is a bookmakers'.

King's Cross Bridge, N1

This sign is relatively new, even though it is somewhat faded. It dates from somewhere between 1984 and 2000, as London Regional Transport were responsible for the public transport system during this period. They took over the responsibility from the Greater London Council, which was officially abolished in 1986.

159 Essex Road, N1

Walking down this portion of Essex Road, most people's eyes are understandably drawn to this ornate former cinema. Opened in 1930 and built in Egyptian-inspired art deco style, it is lavish enough to draw anybody's attention away from the faded advert hiding in the corner.

Though the advert has been cut in half, and is thus difficult to make sense of, it does seem to be advertising dining rooms of some description. Dining rooms are listed at this address from the late 1800s onwards. Arthur Pickering Dining Rooms stood on this spot in 1896 and in 1900 George Hammet set up a hairdressing business here, but in 1906 he added a dining room to his services. By 1926 the business had been taken over by Freeman J.J. & Son Refreshment Rooms.

679 Holloway Road, N19

The crumbling brickwork on the edge of this row reveals a partial advertisement for gold and diamonds. Holloway Road has a history that dates back to the early 1300s; it had become a major thoroughfare by the turn of the twentieth century and was home to numerous pawn and jewellery shops, where local residents and those passing through the city could buy and sell valuable wares. The end of a street, facing the road, is an ideal location for a painted advert, as a large number of passers-by are likely to see it.

266–268 Holloway Road, N7

The Harper Electric Piano Company Ltd was established in May 1910. Two members of the Harper family signed the legal documents to incorporate the company: Sidney Charles, listed as a manufacturer, and Walter, who acted as secretary. They set up shop at Nos 258, 260 and 262 Holloway Road and, according to their business description, were 'dealers and manufacturers of all kinds of automatic musical instruments'.

10 Manor Road, N16

In 1911, local jam maker David Politi built a factory at No.10 Manor Road. By 1921 his family firm, D. Politi & Sons, was manufacturing confectionery and was particularly known for making excellent Turkish delight.

By 1982 the factory occupied Nos 6–12 Manor Road and employed up to 100 people during busy seasons. Some readers may remember their green tins of crème de menthe that proudly sported the N16 postcode.

19 Manor Road, N16

This sign is likely to belong to Harry Thomas & Co., a furniture removal company that occupied this address during the 1930s and '40s. Manor Road boasted several other furniture-related businesses at this time, as the skilled craftsmen who lived in the city during the late 1800s moved further out into Stoke Newington.

7 Wightman Road, N8

The opening of Haringey train station in 1885 meant great expansion for the area. One of the first roads to be laid down by Great Northern Railway was Wightman Road and, understandably, businesses soon set up to exploit passing trade. Thanks to this old signage above the present-day off licence, we know that the Wightman Rd Stores was one such business.

124 Stoke Newington High Street, N16

John Hawkins was a cotton goods manufacturer in the 1930s. The company is listed at a number of addresses, including Chapel Street in Islington, Kilburn High Road and Portobello Road. Though it operated from more than one address, the business essentially kept to the north and west of the city.

13 Northwold Road, N16

This sign for R. Ellis, listed in the early twentieth century under buildings services, betrays the difficulty of accurately dating faded adverts for long-running enterprises. At the bottom of this sign are the words 'est. 60 years'. This could either suggest that businesses routinely painted new adverts even after they were well established, or that the sign was painted earlier and the number of years simply updated as time passed.

129 Holloway Road, N7

This advert is for the Royal Coffee & Dining Rooms. Dining rooms were big business in London in the late 1800s and early 1900s. By 1910 there were over 300 dining rooms listed in the trade directories.

467–469A High Road, N17

O'Meara are a camping company based in Ireland and have been in existence since 1966. This sign was painted sometime in the early 1970s, as during this period it was an O'Meara shop. The business started out in Kilburn in 1959 and moved to Holloway, Kentish Town and Willesden before settling in Tottenham. The shop was sold to Blacks Ltd around 1976.

521 Seven Sisters Road, N15

This extremely faded advert reads: 'Stop Here For The Best Overalls, [Painters?] Blouses, Aprons.' Unusually, the first letter of each word is highlighted in red in order to draw more attention to it for people passing the alleyway in which it appears.

A little further down the alleyway is a sign, complete with manicule, for Herman & Watkins Ltd. The business was mentioned in the *London Gazette* in 1938, when Frederick Ralston Watkins left the partnership. Maurice Herman continued the business alone under the same name, which is listed as a 'Toilet and fancy goods manufacturers'. The company operated from No. 523 Seven Sisters Road.

240 High Street Harlesden, NW10

Prior to being converted into a launderette, this building was a dining room in the 1930s, owned by C. Ferrari. Launderettes are still big business in the capital, as many of the rented studio flats and bedsits do not have room for washing and drying machines.

33 South End Road, NW3

The London and North Eastern Railway operated from 1923 until 1948, after which nationalisation came into effect. The beautiful steam locomotives used by the company were so romantic in their design that they were often used in works of fiction such as *The 39 Steps*, *Get Carter* and, of course, the Harry Potter films. This advert, however, reminds us that the engines were designed to be fast as well as ornate.

4

SOUTH LONDON

195–205 Union Street, SE1

James Ashby established himself as a wholesale tea dealer in 1850. He imported and packaged teas from all over the world.

In the 1930s and 1940s the business was listed at several addresses, including Marshalsea Road and Idol Lane.

Rose Brand Fine Teas were one of the many brands listed in Ashby & Sons' portfolio. The company still exists today as Ashbys of London Teas. This building was reportedly scheduled for demolition in 2008 but, for now, is still standing.

66 The Cut, SE1

Behind the signage for the Young Vic Theatre in Southwark is an old sign for Wilson Bros, a chain of butchers. In 1936 the company had a shop at this address, although at that time it was known as No. 52 The New Cut.

Wilson Bros was a fairly substantial chain and also had shops on Uxbridge Road, Northcote Road and in Shepherd's Bush.

57 Bermondsey Street, SE1

Thomson Bros Ltd is listed in the early 1940s as paper merchants, dry-cleaners and general paper bag makers. The company's registered evacuation address is Central Parade, St Mark's Hill, Surbiton. Seemingly, they were moved out of central London during wartime in order to continue the manufacturing of paper, which was an important material at this time.

3–4 Weston Street, SE1

The Bermondsey area of London is well known for producing leather. M. Emanuel was one of the many merchants to work in the leather market, alongside William Langley & Co., Hyde & Skin Merchants and Booth & Co. leather manufacturers.

135 Evelina Road, SE15

Lipton Tea was founded by Glasgow-born Sir Thomas Lipton in 1893. Just like other successful entrepreneurs of the era, such as King C. Gillette and William Lever, his success in the tea trade was based on the ideal of making the product accessible and affordable for the masses. His company was an instant success and earned him a knighthood from Queen Victoria in 1898.

74 Southwark Bridge Road, SE1

When Southwark Bridge was opened in 1819, a thoroughfare connecting Borough Street and Blackfriars Road was also established. The new Southwark Bridge Road brought an increase of trade and traffic, and consequently the population of the area doubled between 1801 and 1851. Businesses such as R. Sullivan's wardrobe dealers would have no doubt seized on this increase in footfall.

Sullivan's was clearly not the first business to hand paint a sign here, as other lettering shows up behind theirs, though it is too faint to read.

It also looks as though the buildings may have been renumbered, as the number eight is clearly visible, though faded, behind Sullivan's numbering.

115 St John's Hill, SW11

Alongside Hovis and Daren, Peterkin is now a subsidiary of Rank Hovis McDougall. Peterkin flour and custard were launched by Joseph Arthur Rank before he made a name for himself in the film industry. As he was already screening and making films by the early 1930s, this advert is likely to have been painted in the 1910s or '20s.

76–78 Denmark Hill, SE5

John Haig & Co. are listed in the 1930s as whisky blenders. The head office was based at Distillers House, No. 21 James Square. The slogan in blue at the bottom claims that Haig & Co. is the oldest Scotch whisky distillers in the world.

113 Bellenden Road, SE15

Although this advert boasts that Cutts & Co. was established in 1884, the signage does not date back that far. The company only moved to this address in 1940, meaning that it was painted sometime after that. Before 1940 it was based at No. 20 Victoria Road in Peckham. The company lasted into the 1950s.

17 The Pavement, SW4

Deane & Co. Chemists is listed at No. 17 The Pavement in historical business directories. According to the company's prescription books and accounts, they were dispensing medicines between 1910 and 1973. This advert is well preserved, which may mean it was either painted quite late or repainted over the time the business was in operation.

48 Battersea Rise, SW11

This advert promotes both the *National News* and the *Sunday Evening Telegram*, the first evening newspaper in Britain. Unlike a lot of the other adverts in this volume, dating this sign is fairly simple as the *Sunday Evening Telegram* only existed between 1917 and 1921. The *National News* ultimately became the *Sunday Illustrated*.

18 Electric Lane, SW9

Our Sons Ltd Clothiers is listed at
Nos 18, 20 and 22 Electric Avenue in
the 1930s. Next door was a listing for
Our Ladies Clothiers, indicating that
the shop catered for both male and
female customers.

The business didn't survive beyond the
1940s, but from the sign it is clear that
they stocked quite a substantial range of
brands, including Dexer, Jantzen, Bukta
and Tootal.

10A Sunnyhill Road, SW16

This advert has two layers but, due to the vibrancy of the Portogram layer, it is impossible to read what was advertised underneath. The faded slogan at the bottom of this advert reads: 'Spans The World.'

18 Upper Tooting Road, SW17

This pharmacy is still trading under the name of Nettles and has been for decades. Meggezones are pastilles designed to relieve cold and flu symptoms and have been on the market for over thirty years. This advert is likely to have been painted when they first became available in order to boost initial product sales.

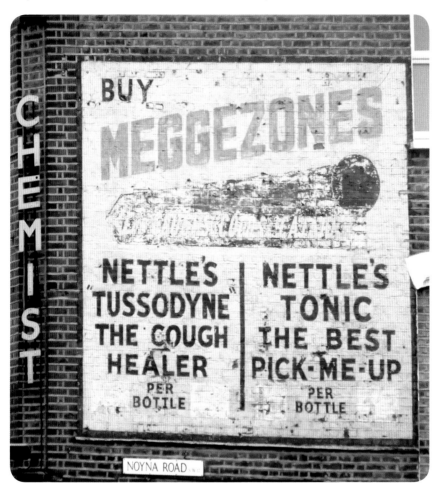

49 Tooting High Street, SW17

This advert is difficult to see from the ground, but either a ride down Tooting High Street on a double-decker bus or a browse in old business directories confirms that this is a sign for Perry & Son. In the 1930s they owned a jewellers at No. 49 and a pawnbrokers at No. 90 Tooting High Street.

78 Merton High Street, SW19

Cliff's Corner was a corner shop that has long since closed. Looking closely at the advert, there is some lettering underneath Cliff's sign, possibly the word 'Tea'. This building is situated on an old parade of shops that is currently uninhabited.

5

EAST LONDON

118 Northwold Road, E5

Strongs Butchers Ltd were listed at this address in the 1940s and were clearly keen to emphasise the quality of their meat to customers with this prominent advert on the main road. The building has since been converted into a private residence.

50–52 Brushfield Street, E1

Percy Dalton's Peanut Company was established in the 1930s by the Dalton family. The peanuts are still on sale, but went through a rebranding in 2012 that made the packaging very different from the original concept.

The Old Peanut Factory, E3

The old peanut factory still stands, juxtaposed with the new Olympic Park in Hackney, but is no longer used for the production or distribution of peanuts – it has been transformed into trendy flats for creatives working in the area.

46 Crispin Street, E1

Although it seems as though the Donovan Bros worked at this address, they are actually listed in business directories at their paper bag factory, which was on Sclater Street, near Bishopsgate. Their product clearly was sold at this address, however, as a Mrs Deborah Levington worked here in the 1930s as a paper bag dealer.

108 Commercial Street, E1

The 1891 census reveals that twenty-six-year-old William Wakefield, originally from the Spitalfields area, worked at this address as a market salesman. He was accompanied by twenty-four-year-old assistant saleswoman Esther Ann Wakefield and thirty-year-old Archie Wakefield, an assistant salesman. Esther and Archie both hailed from Essex.

428 Hackney Road, E2

John Tann Ltd was established in 1795. According to the business listings in the 1930s the company specialised in safes, strong rooms, doors and safe deposits, cash and deed boxes and locks. Although this sign is on Hackney Road, the business operated from No. 117 Newgate Street. It is also listed at St Stephen's Road during this time.

201 Whitechapel Road, E1

Whitechapel Road is famous for three things: Jack the Ripper, The Blind Beggar (the pub where Ronnie Kray shot George Cornell in 1966) and being the cheapest property, alongside Old Kent Road, on the original Monopoly board. A less-known feature are these old adverts for Bedding, Bedsteads, Feathers and Flocks, but given Whitechapel Road's notorious characters, who knows who bought their duvets there?

106 Brick Lane, E1

When buildings frequently change use, as this one has, layers of advertisements for goods and services build up. Sometimes adverts have been overwritten so many times that it becomes difficult to decipher the layers and read what is there. Barely legible on this example is the word 'Bernard's'.

Luckily the same advert is mirrored on the other side of the building and is not as faded. The words 'Hosiery' and 'Hatter' are legible here. This building

was used by Sydney Moss in 1915 who was a hosier. In 1895 it was used by grocers Dubowski Barnett & Sons, but is now a newsagents.

The Old Truman Brewery, 152C Brick Lane, E1

Truman's was established on Brick Lane in 1666. The company prided itself on producing beer in the East End and being a truly independent brewer. In 1989, however, a merger took place that saw the brewery and the pubs sold.

147 Brick Lane, E1

Tiles such as this example can be found on buildings all over London, advertising the Truman brand name and products. Truman's relaunched in 2010 and bought a new brewery in Hackney Wick, just a short distance from the original Truman heritage on Brick Lane.

478 Kingsland Road, E8

In addition to the lettering for Gillette and a former cafe, this wall also advertises the *Sunday Illustrated*. As mentioned on page 60, the *Sunday Illustrated* was once the *National News*. It was founded by Horatio Bottomley, who was MP for South Hackney. Sadly the publication only lasted a few years due to high production costs.

134 Kingsland Road, E2

This advert is so admired within the local community that it has been granted a local listing. This simply means that the council must think about the impact any planning decisions they make may have on the advert. This is good news as it is unlikely the building will be demolished or that the sign will be obscured by another building.

Royal Mint Street, E1

This hydraulic power tower stands on its own near Royal Mint Street. The faded lettering is almost too weak to decipher but an earlier photograph confirms it once said the following: 'London Midland & Scottish Railway City Goods Station and Bonded Stores.'

148 Narrow Street, E14

J. & R. Wilson & Co. were listed in the 1930s as ship chandlers, ship's store and general export merchants. Their main business was selling materials that are useful for ships and sailing. They were listed both at this address and at No. 3 New London Street.

1 Pennyfields, E14

Finding this old signage for the London Docklands Development Corporation requires rooting through the bushes opposite the shops at Pennyfields. Though the sign is faded, it's not as old as it might look, as the corporation operated between 1981 and 1998. It was a quango designed to regenerate the Docklands area, particularly focusing on improving job prospects and housing.

6

WEST LONDON

Hammersmith Tube Station, W6

Wait for the trains to depart on the Hammersmith & City line at Hammersmith Tube Station and an old advert for the Hammersmith Palais de Danse will be revealed.

The Palais de Danse operated as a music venue and dance hall between 1919 and 2007. The iconic building was sadly demolished in May 2012.

Now that the building is gone, all that physically remains of the Palais de Danse is this advert, which boasts of 'twice daily' dances at affordable prices.

Q-Park Poland Street, W1F

Just inside the entrance to this gloomy Soho car park are two well-preserved adverts. Promoting car oil and tyres on the way into a car park is somewhat savvy, but, as an additional perk, the building has protected these two adverts from the elements, keeping them in excellent condition.

63 Great Titchfield Street, W1W

J.H. Pepperell, the fruiterer and greengrocers, were listed at this address in Fitzrovia in the 1940s. This is a major street between Oxford Street and Goodge Street and consequently a great many potential customers pass through every day, and have done for decades.

This area of London was not very prosperous in the mid-nineteenth century but, by the turn of the century, a redevelopment took place. Old houses were torn down and comparatively luxurious apartments were put up in their place.

The street is now considered part of the garment district – which has expanded from nearby Soho – and is home to many creative and media firms that have moved into the area.

58 Richmond Way, W14

This advert for an old dairy is so faded that it is somewhat difficult to decipher. The name A.C. Creswell can just be seen. The advert suggests that the dairy was also a bakery as the word 'pastrycook' is evident at the top of the sign, and at the bottom it claims the business is 'noted for homemade bread'.

56 Shepherd's Bush Green, W12

The Shepherd's Bush Cinematograph Theatre was built in 1910 and originally seated 900 people. On opening, however, there were problems with the local power supply and consequently the building reopened in 1923 as the New Palladium.

The cinema went through several incarnations, including the Essoldo, the Classic, and the Odeon 2. Like most vanished cinemas it suffered greatly during the admissions slump of the late 1970s and early '80s, closing its doors in 1981.

It was eventually converted into a pub and is now owned by bar chain Walkabout. The signage on the site, located at the side of the building, and its intricate arching lines are now the only hints of its earlier heritage.

19 Langley Drive, W4

This advert for R.J. Hewett Ltd is oddly situated on the side of a private residence, suggesting a commercial to residential conversion at some stage. Though company-founder Richard Hewett died in 1935, the company continued on into the 1960s.

206 Acton Lane, W4

Spratt's was an animal food company, particularly known for its patented dog biscuits. This advert is for A.H. Payne, who sold Spratt's products such as dog, poultry and caged-bird food.

39b George Street, TW9

The muted shades of this old advert for hair colouring suggests that at one time it would have been painted in vibrant shades, but that the paint has since worn away.

George Street has long been the social and economic hub in Richmond. In the 1600s stocks were located just at the back of this building, and the occasional hanging was staged there too. After its life as a hairdresser, this building was taken over by high-end retail brands and in recent history has housed both Karen Millen and Jack Wills stores.

7 Sheen Road, TW9

In many respects the adverts in this volume are a reminder of the independent businesses that used to thrive before large chains took over the high street. Businesses such as A.B. Abbett – shown in this photograph – are more difficult to come by in modern towns.

This modest marker for the bakery is placed in the window which was probably once crammed with mouth-watering cakes and pastries. Although difficult to see at a glance, anyone who stopped to look in the window would be reminded of the business name.

Many businesses from earlier decades seem keen to embed their location into their advertising and signage. This is partly to remind people where to go when they want to spend money, but may also suggest there was a sense of local pride and that customers were potentially more likely to buy from local stores.

82–86 Sheen Road, TW9

The location of this particular advert seems odd in comparison to the others in this volume. It is situated on the back of a house on a quiet street. There is, however, a railway line on the other side of the main road, and perhaps the original hope was that local residents would notice the sign on their way to the train station. Another explanation could be that the layout of the roads was different when the sign was originally painted.

52 High Street Hampton, TW12

Drapery stores such as this one are also more difficult to find in the twenty-first century. The onus now is on large warehouse stores that offer all homeware under one roof. Looking at this collection as a whole, it is difficult to resist the idea that much of the individuality that these adverts convey had become lost by the second half of the twentieth century.

7

IMITATION
RESTORATION
PRESERVATION

Queen's Yard, White Post Lane, E9

Vintage brands are currently experiencing a resurgence in popularity and consequently faded adverts are being imitated, restored and preserved in a range of different ways.

These two adverts in Queen's Yard are actually part of a mural project that celebrates the industrial heritage of the Hackney area. If they're still in existence in fifty years it would be quite easy for onlookers to confuse the faded murals with authentic adverts.

181 Upper Street, N1

Businesses are also cashing in on the quaint appeal of shabby chic signage. This sign for a pub on Upper Street looks old but has only been in place for a few years.

35 Putney Bridge Road, SW18

With the Queen Adelaide pub in Putney it's difficult to tell whether or not the owners simply haven't had time to update their sign or whether they're deliberately allowing this advert to fade. Either way, it possesses a certain nostalgic charm, even though it is relatively new.

312 Archway Road, N6

Even big brands such as Jack Daniels have acknowledged the allure of age and vintage. Most of their advertising messages are built around the longevity of their brand and now they have produced the faded signage to match their television and billboard output.

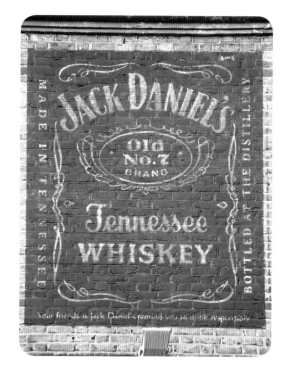

4 Stepney Green, E1

There is a great deal of controversy over whether or not fading adverts should be restored. This sign for Daren bread is much clearer than the others because it has been repainted and, on a positive note, it is possible to deduce from this how some of the other Daren signs may have once looked.

50 High Road, NW10

This advert for Saint Paul's Pianos has also been restored and some enthusiasts argue that this simply changes the old sign into a new sign. It no longer has the faded charm and there is also the issue of whether or not exactly the correct colours and fonts are used. In many respects, when a sign is repainted it becomes a reproduction rather than a historical artefact.

336 Norwood Road, SE27

Many enthusiasts for old painted adverts are infuriated by billboards covering up signs that they would like to photograph and catalogue. This Brymay sign, however, has clearly benefited from the protection of billboards, which is why it is still very readable.

2 Goldhawk Road, W12

The same cannot be said of this Brymay sign in Shepherd's Bush. It is obvious, looking at this sign, how the covering of hoarding or billboards can sometimes be a good thing. Given the state of this advert and some others around London, a growing number of people are interested in preserving these signs for future generations to appreciate.

York Parade, Great West Road, TW8

If vintage adverts are built of letter plates rather than hand painted onto brick, preservation is made easier. This famous Lucozade sign in Brentford is actually a replacement of the original sign that once graced the M4.

The real Lucozade advert is safely inside Gunnersbury Park Museum, where it can be preserved and, simultaneously, enjoyed. In many respects this is the ideal situation in terms of preservation.

96–98 Bishop's Bridge Road, W2

Mosaic and tile signage wears much better than hand-painted adverts too. This mosaic from the Queens Cinema in Bayswater has survived since 1932. It has probably been covered over at some point, given that the cinema closed down in 1988, but it is still in remarkable condition. The building no longer exists, but the frontage remains.

14 Carteret Street, WC2N

This mosaic is another example of a well-preserved advert, although the mystery of its cultural or industrial significance has yet to be solved. Unverified accounts have suggested that it is either an advert for a cigarette brand, or that it marked the site where the Victor Talking Machine was produced.

19–21 Station Parade, TW9

If hand-painted adverts are not preserved, they are usually destroyed without a thought. This sign for a cafe in Kew is now unreadable.

86 Stoke Newington High Street, N16

Thankfully this advert for Cakebread Robey & Co. builders' merchants survived this construction work, but there are no guarantees it will survive the next round of scaffolding unless more people are made aware of the social importance of these adverts. The company is listed as wholesale ironmongers, glass, colour and builders' merchants at this address in 1936. The business was also known as stained-glass artists and lead glaziers. They no doubt crafted some beautiful creations and consequently it only seems right to preserve any reminder of the contribution this manufacturer made to early twentieth-century industry.

113 Stoke Newington Church Street, N16

When it comes to preserving hand-painted signs, the best course of action is to petition for an official local listing. This sign has acquired a listing and the council now have to take the advert's preservation into account when making planning decisions. The L.E. Waterman Co. was listed as a fountain pen manufacturer in the 1930s. Appropriately, the company's address was Pen Corner, No. 41 Kingsway. Similarly, the Walker Bros were listed at this address at the same time, as stationers. They were no longer listed here by the end of the Second World War but, thanks to the listing status on this advert, their legacy will live on.

BIBLIOGRAPHY

Books

Beaver, Patrick, *The Match Makers: The Story of Bryant & May* (Henry Melland, 1985)

Bunford, Caroline & Phil, *Liverpool Ghost Signs* (The History Press, 2012)

De Vries, Tjitte & Mul, Ati, *'They Thought it was a Marvel': Arthur Melbourne-Cooper (1874–1961), Pioneer of Puppet Animation* (Pallas Publications, 2010)

Drury, E. & Lewis, P., *Forgotten London: A Picture of Life in the 1920s* (Batsford, 2011)

Evans, W.A., *Advertising Today and Tomorrow* (Routledge, 2013)

Gray, Richard, *Cinemas in Britain: One Hundred Years of Cinema Architecture* (Lund Humphries Publishers Ltd, 1996)

Roberts, Sam, *Hand-Painted Signs of Kratie* (Ghostsigns, 2012)

Post Office London Directories from the years 1896, 1901, 1906, 1912, 1915, 1925, 1926, 1936, 1937, 1940, 1941, 1954 and 1965

Websites

amwell.org.uk/history

andrewwhitehead.net

bbc.co.uk

britishcinemagreats.com

british-history.ac.uk

britishpathe.com

census1891.com

dakotaboo-in-search-of-space.blogspot.co.uk

derelictlondon.com

faded-london.blogspot.co.uk

ghostsigns.co.uk

herberthistory.co.uk

historicaldirectories.org

hounslowchronicle.co.uk

hydonian.blogspot.co.uk

independent.co.uk

janeslondon.com

islington.gov.uk

liptontea.com

literarylondon.org

London-gazette.co.uk

nationalarchives.gov.uk

nestle-family.com

nj.com

nytimes.com

omearacamping.com

richmond.gov.uk

paintedsignsandmosaics.blogspot.co.uk

scatesconcertinas.com

scotlandmag.com

search.freefind.com

subbrit.org.uk

the-walls-have-ears.tumblr.com

trumansbeer.co.uk

unilever.com